UNEXPLORED

C.PLAN 5 2/2/04

UNINTERESTING

BLE

COALM...

PLEASE NOTE!

CATS BELIEVE IN NINE LIVES
THROUGH WHICH THEY PROGRESS.
AFTER THE LAST LIFE THEY
ARRIVE AT CAT ENLIGHTENMENT
WHERE THEY RECEIVE A REWARD.
PRESUMABLY FOOD.

Jim –
THE NINE LIVES OF A DYSFUNCTIONAL CAT

by Steven Appleby

BLOOMSBURY

For Jim.

Special thanks to Nicola Sherring for suggesting Jim do a book.

Thanks also to: Nick Battey; Lisa Birdwood; Pete Bishop; Jonny Boatfield; Adam Boome; Karen Brown; Liz Calder; Rosemary Davidson; Mary Tomlinson; Gabrielle Walker & Matt Willis-Jones.

First published 2003.

Bloomsbury Publishing PLC,
38 Soho Square, London W1D 3HB.

ISBN 0 7475 6935 5.

Printed in Great Britain by Bath Press.

I am the centre
of the universe.

An Introduction to Jim

IT IS A DAY LIKE ANY OTHER AND JIM THE CAT
STARES ACROSS THE GARDEN TOWARDS THE
EDGE OF THE WORLD.

THIS IS WHAT HE IS THINKING:

The world exists purely for me.

It is a test.

The world is made up of moving things, stationary things and me.

I must journey through it, learning and acquiring wisdom, until I pass into the next world.

At which point this world will cease to exist!

JIM APPEARS QUITE CONTENT, BUT INSIDE HE
FEELS VAGUELY DISSATISFIED. SOME
UNANSWERED QUESTIONS LURK IN THE
CORNERS OF HIS MIND, REFUSING TO GO AWAY.

Why is there never a place set for me at the dinner table?

Why has no one given me a set of clothes or a pair of pyjamas?

Why don't I have my own room like the other members of my family?

AS USUAL, CONFRONTING THESE THOUGHTS
MAKES JIM FEEL TIRED.
SOON HE FALLS FAST ASLEEP...

It is simpler
to be a possession.

JIM

JIM'S LIVES...

No. 1 ~ SLOTH.

No. 2 ~ LOVE.

No. 3 ~ ENVY.

No. 4 ~ GLUTTONY.

No. 5 ~ VANITY.

No. 6 ~ DISHONESTY.

No. 7 ~ DEBAUCHERY.

No. 8 ~ CONTRITION.

No. 9 ~ STUPIDITY.

Life no. 1 ~ SLOTH

In which Jim does absolutely nothing at all.

HERE WE SEE JUST A FEW OF THE NINETY-NINE BASIC POSITIONS:

fig a ~ ON THE SOFA.

fig b ~ ON THE CLEAN WASHING.

fig c ~ ON A FLOWER.

fig d ~ WHEREVER YOU ARE ABOUT TO SIT.

fig e ~ IN THE WAY.

fig f ~ BEHIND YOUR HEAD.

Does Jim have fleas at the moment?

fig g ~ ON A TEATOWEL.

fig h ~ SNUGGLED UP TO THE TEAPOT.

Cosy...

fig i ~ IN THE VEGETABLE CUPBOARD.

fig j ~ ON ANY ITEM OF CLOTHING LEFT OUT FOR JUST A MINUTE.

My new jumper!

fig k ~ IN THE PRAM.

fig l ~ SOME OF THE EVIDENCE JIM LEAVES BEHIND.

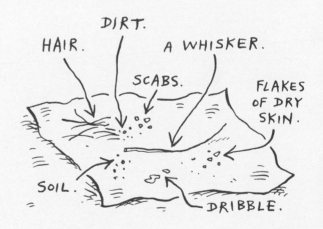

DIRT.

HAIR.

A WHISKER.

SCABS.

FLAKES OF DRY SKIN.

SOIL.

DRIBBLE.

What's happening? I
seem to be having
an out-of-cat
experience!

FLOAT

17

Look. Jim's fine!
I really thought he'd stopped breathing for a moment there.
miaow...

Life no. 2 ~ LOVE

In which Jim comes upon the double-edged sword of LOVE — and cuts himself extremely badly.

Love... Now, THERE's a worthy calling!

Love is pure...

Mnngh!

Platonic!

Chivalrous...

Hard work!

Yes, I think I'll devote myself to love.

20

LET'S WATCH AND LEARN AS JIM BEGINS HIS QUEST FOR LOVE...

1 - RUB AGAINST LEGS.

2 - PURR LOUDLY.

3 - NUZZLE HAND.

4 - LIFT CHIN FOR TICKLING.

5 - CLOSE EYES ECSTATICALLY.

6 - JUMP ONTO KNEE.

7 — PURR LIKE A TRACTOR.

Poo! His breath's a bit strong!

WRRR... WRRR...

8 — GAZE UP AFFECTIONATELY.

UGH! There are ghastly knobbly lumps under his fur!

Cysts, I think.

9 — CLAW KNEES LOVINGLY.

Anyway, he's SO affectionate, aren't you, Jim? OUCH!

10 — CRAWL TOWARDS FACE.

Ah, a lovely cup of tea. Thank you.

11 — CLING ON TIGHTLY.

Hop down, Jim, while I drink my tea.

12 — DIG CLAWS IN FIRMLY.

I said down. DOWN! Oh, he's up again.

Biscuit?

miaow!

22

13 – LET YOURSELF BE STROKED. IT CALMS THEM.

You're a lovely boy, but enough's enough.

14 – LOYALLY HEAD-BUTT HAND.

You've spilt my tea! GET DOWN!

15 – SHOW THEM YOU CARE.

He's clinging on gamely... DAMN! He's pulled my jumper!

16 – MIAOW SEDUCTIVELY.

Shoo, Jim! Off you go!

17 – HANG ABOUT WATCHING FOR AN OPENING.

If you stand up he'll get discouraged and go away.

Good idea.

18 – NEVER GIVE UP.

Don't look at him!

19 ~ RUN AND JUMP.

I'll shut him out in the garden. Come on, Jim.

20 ~ GAZE BESEECHINGLY TO MAKE THEM OPEN THE DOOR AGAIN.

He's a super cat, though.

Yes, we all love him dearly.

THEN SUDDENLY!

Well, hello... big boy!

Hu... Hu... Hu...

SOON <u>LOVE</u> WAS JOINED BY SEXUAL <u>LUST</u>!

25

THE KNOWLEDGE THAT HE HAS BEEN 'DONE' SHOCKS JIM TO THE CORE. HE IS TORTURED BY FEELINGS OF INADEQUACY. DESPERATELY HE TURNS TO HIS FAMILY FOR SUPPORT.

REJECTED, JIM STUMBLES OUTSIDE.

27

Life no. 3 — ENVY

In which Jim wants, wants, wants and ends up getting more than he deserves...

Here we go again...

THIS IS WHERE JIM THINKS HE BELONGS
IN THE FAMILY PECKING ORDER:

WHERE HE ACTUALLY IS:

31

SOME OF THE HOPES AND DESIRES JIM DREAMS ABOUT:

RESENTFULLY, JIM SETTLES DOWN IN ONE OF HIS FAVOURITE SPOTS FOR A SNOOZE.

Don't dream! What a cheek! In fact, I'm dreaming right now... zZZzZZzzzz

Here I am at the controls of the Appleby family estate!

33

Well, you were wrong there.

I sure was.

You won't do that again...

YAWN...

I dream, therefore I am... Or do I dream? And am I?

Life no. 4 ～ GLUTTONY

In which Jim becomes just desert.

Odd. My plate's on the floor. Again!

And they seem to have forgotten to set me a place at the table.

Mmm. That butter looks tasty... I'll just take my share...

GET OFF THE TABLE, YOU BRUTE!!

Yummy!

37

JIM CAN'T UNDERSTAND WHY HE ISN'T ALLOWED TO EAT AT THE TABLE WITH THE REST OF HIS FAMILY.

Their food always smells more interesting than mine.

I'll go and get some human food elsewhere...

JIM SNEAKS INTO NUMBER SIXTY-THREE AND STEALS A STEAK WHICH MRS BLOATER HAS JUST COOKED FOR HER HUSBAND'S SUPPER.

It's ready!

Coming!

THE NEXT MORNING HE COMES BACK AND STEALS TWO RASHERS OF BACON FROM HER FRYING PAN.

OVER THE NEXT WEEK JIM PINCHES A MEATBALL, A SLICE OF CAKE, A HAM SANDWICH, SEVEN CHIPS, SOME SPAGHETTI AND A CHICKEN LEG.

JIM WILL EAT ANYTHING.

BUT MRS BLOATER HAS CAUGHT ON...

Enough is ENOUGH!

I'm going to put a stop to all this thieving!

Bloody cat!

SHE TRIES TO FLATTEN JIM WITH A MALLET. SHE TRIES TO DROWN HIM IN THE SINK. SHE TRIES TO SQUEEZE HIM BEHIND THE KITCHEN DOOR. SHE EVEN TRIES TO SHUT HIM IN THE FREEZER.

AAARGH!!

AS THE DAYS TURN INTO WEEKS, MRS BLOATER'S FURY SMOULDERS INTO OBSESSION AND THEN MADNESS.

Grrrr...

zzzzz

EVENTUALLY SHE COMES UP WITH THE PERFECT TRAP.

SHE SEASONS A CHOP WITH ARSENIC AND LEAVES IT SIMMERING ON THE COOKER TOP.

TO MAKE SURE NOTHING SCARES JIM OFF, SHE GOES OUT TO THE SHOP.

NO SOONER HAS SHE LEFT THAN JIM JUMPS IN THROUGH THE OPEN KITCHEN WINDOW.

UNFORTUNATELY, MR BLOATER ARRIVES HOME UNEXPECTEDLY AND CHASES JIM AWAY WITH A MOP.

GRRRR...

HE THEN DEVOURS THE CHOP HIMSELF.

40

AFTER THE FUNERAL, AT WHICH JIM STOLE SOME PRAWNS, MRS BLOATER RESOLVES TO GET EVEN.

SHE DECIDES TO TRY A DIFFERENT APPROACH.

DAY TWO ~

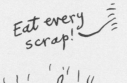

DAY THREE ~

DAY FOUR ~

DAY FIVE ~

41

JIM'S FAVOURITE PLACES TO BE SICK:

i — ON THE KITCHEN TABLE.

ii — ON THE COOKERY BOOKS.

iii — ON A NOVEL, ON SOME CDs OR ON TODAY'S NEWSPAPER.

iv — IN A DARK CORNER WHERE THE SICK CAN LIE UNDISTURBED FOR WEEKS.

v — ON THE DOORMAT.

vi — ON A CHAIR.

NOT FORGETTING: ON THE SWIMMING THINGS; IN A HANDBAG; ON THE BATHMAT; ON YOUR PILLOW; ON SOME UNFINISHED HOMEWORK.

DAY SIX —

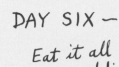
Eat it all or no pudding!

BELCH!

DAY SEVEN —

Clean your plate, now!

DAY EIGHT —

Yum yum! Eighty-two beefburgers!

TWITCH!

THUD!

DAY NINE —

Now it's <u>MY</u> turn!

Cat pie — fair's fair!

Damn! He won't fit in the oven!

Phew! It's nice to feel light again!
You don't LOOK light.
I'm still sexually aroused.
YAWN...
Back I go...
WADDLE...

I'm going to find a
nice quiet garden,
settle down and...

JIMS FAVOURITE SPOTS TO HAVE A POO:

i — IN THE FLOWERBED.

ii — IN THE BARK CHIPPINGS UNDERNEATH THE SWING.

iii — IN A NEIGHBOUR'S GARDEN.

Ugh!

iv — IN THE SANDPIT.

v — ON THE PATH.

Jim's a good cat. He never poos in the house.

Of course not. That's DISGUSTING!

Life no. 5 — VANITY

In which Jim is dressed to kill... or be killed.

THE CHILDREN KNEW
THAT A CAT WITHOUT A
HAT IS LIKE A YO-YO
WITHOUT STRING.
A POINTLESS THING.

I bet we can find
that poor cat a
hat! I bet we can!

Cats wear hats.
It says so in a
book.

JIM LAY ON THE WALL
AND STARED ACROSS THE
GARDEN, EYES HALF SHUT,
WATCHING FLIES.

We'll call you BEAN!
No, SPROUT!

No, MR
MACLEAN!

49

SUDDENLY...

50

JIM HEARS THE SOUND OF A CAR PULLING AWAY.

THE DAYS PASS SLOWLY. AND THE NIGHTS...

VERY SLOWLY.

UNTIL...

At last!
That was
boring.

Ciao, everybody!

Life no. 6 — DISHONESTY

In which Jim learns to be duplicitous.

SO JIM GOES SNOOPING —
OR RESEARCHING, AS HE
PREFERS TO CALL IT.

HE LEARNS THAT THE
LADY IN NUMBER
SIXTY-SIX TELLS FIBS...

Yes, of course I've got a TV licence!

AND THE BOY AT
NUMBER TWENTY-TWO...

Have you just eaten nineteen iced buns?!

BELCH!

No.

AND THE MAN FROM
NUMBER TWELVE.

It's fine. My wife and I have an open marriage.

Okay, Bob.

58

AND WHEN THE SCRABBLE BOARD COMES OUT AFTER SUPPER THERE IS ANOTHER MESSAGE.

LATER THAT NIGHT...

61

Life no. 7 ~ DEBAUCHERY

In which Jim goes downhill more rapidly than one would believe possible, except in a book.

I need a stiff drink!

That's what a human would do after a shock like mine, anyway.

LATER.

Whole... pack's... gone...

HIC!

Look at Jim!

He's a disgrace!

He STINKS of booze!

Out you go! You can sober up outside!

LATER, IN A DIRTY ALLEYWAY...

EVENTUALLY JIM SOBERS UP AND STAGGERS HOME.

SHORTLY.

BUT AN HOUR LATER...

IF <u>YOUR</u> CAT DISAPPEARS
FOR DAYS ON END,
READER, BE WARNED!
HE'S PROBABLY ON A
BENDER, LIKE JIM.

We haven't seen Jim for days, Mum.

Is he alright?

Not really, dear. It's very sad.

"Should we pray for him, Mummy?"

PATHETIC CRAWL...

"You could try, dear, but I don't think it would help. You see, cats aren't important to God. Not like humans."

"So I don't think he's likely to answer a prayer for a cat, do you?"

SLUMP!

"No, Mummy."

Then can we get a new pet? I'd like a canary!

um, we'll see...

I'd like an elephant!

You're still drunk!
Poo! Whisky breath!
Ghostly booze doesn't pack the same punch, though...
BELCH!
YAWN...
I'm hungry again minutes after eating ghostly food.
Oooh...

Life no. 8 — CONTRITION

In which Jim appears to have learnt his lesson, but...

70

I'm even quite glad to see my bowl...

Though I'd still be happier if it was on the table.

JUMBO
JIM

I want this life to last a bit longer, so I'm going to turn over a new leaf.

Goodnight, Jim!

GA!

No more drinking and smoking.

No stealing from the neighbours.

I'm going to keep my nose out of other people's business.

I'm going to help around the house.

And I'm not going to waste this life sleeping.

71

AND I'm going to iron my own clothes!
HISSSS...
There we are.
And now, time for bed.
YAWN...

IN NO
TIME
AT ALL...

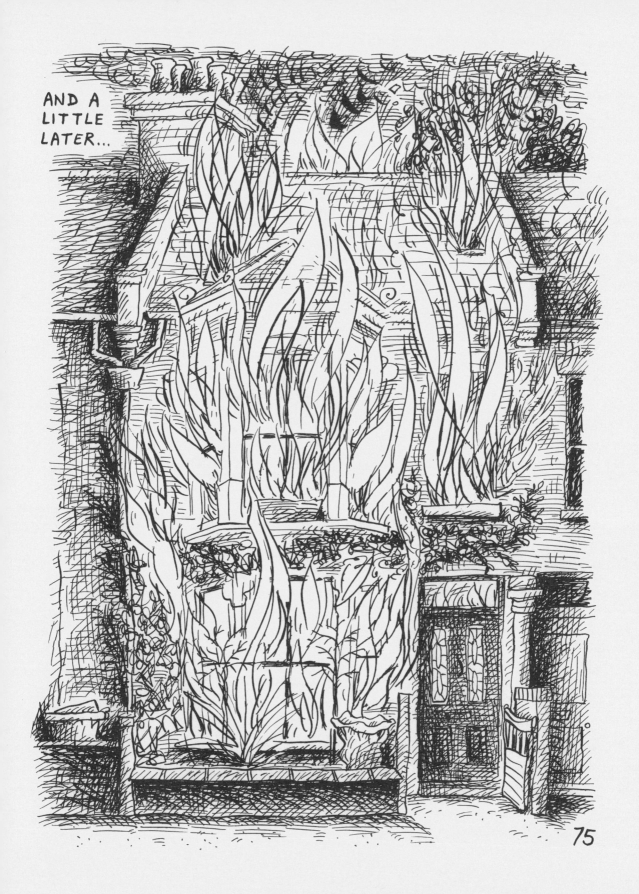

AND A
LITTLE
LATER...

75

Life no. 9 ~ STUPIDITY

In which Jim completes the test and the world comes to an end...

Jim survived!

HURRAH!

Here I am, back in the good old world, quite content to be a cat and ready to live to a happy old age.

LATER, IN THE FAMILY'S TEMPORARY HOME.

Hmm... I feel compelled to sit on this newspaper.

ELEPHANT BEDDING.

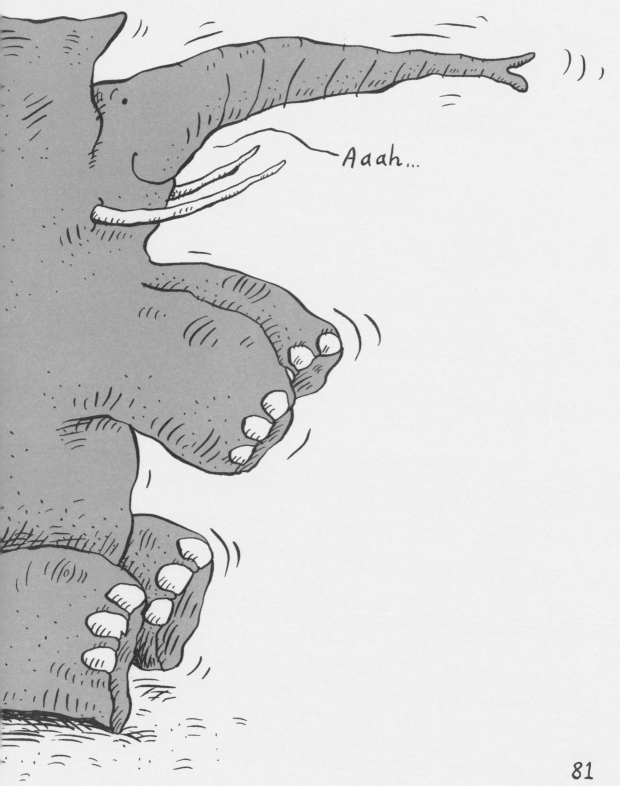

Aaah...

So I really WAS
the centre of
the universe!

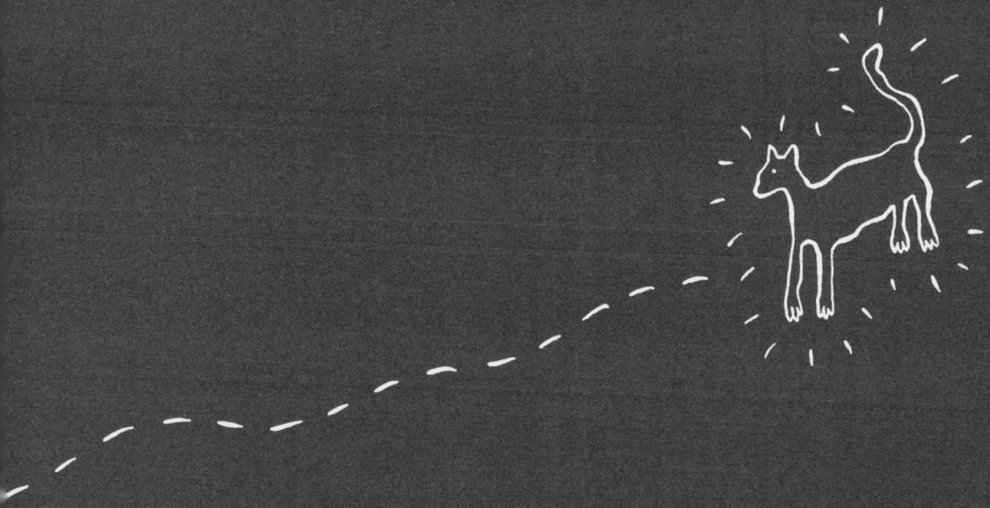

Hello, guys.
At last!
What happens now?
Perhaps I'll come back as a human...
Is there another life?

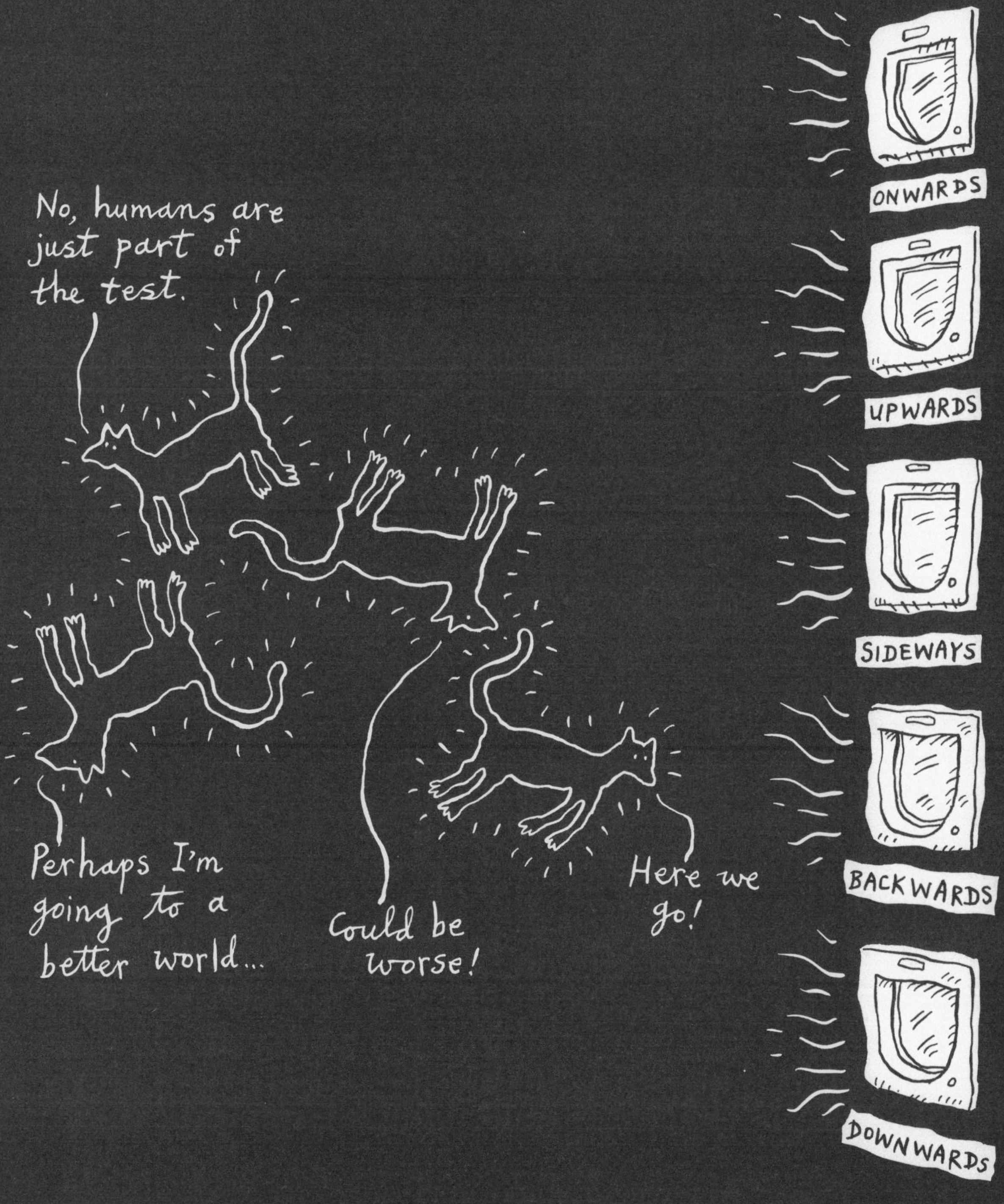
No, humans are just part of the test.
Perhaps I'm going to a better world...
Could be worse!
Here we go!
ONWARDS
UPWARDS
SIDEWAYS
BACKWARDS
DOWNWARDS

The REAL Jim.

The End ?

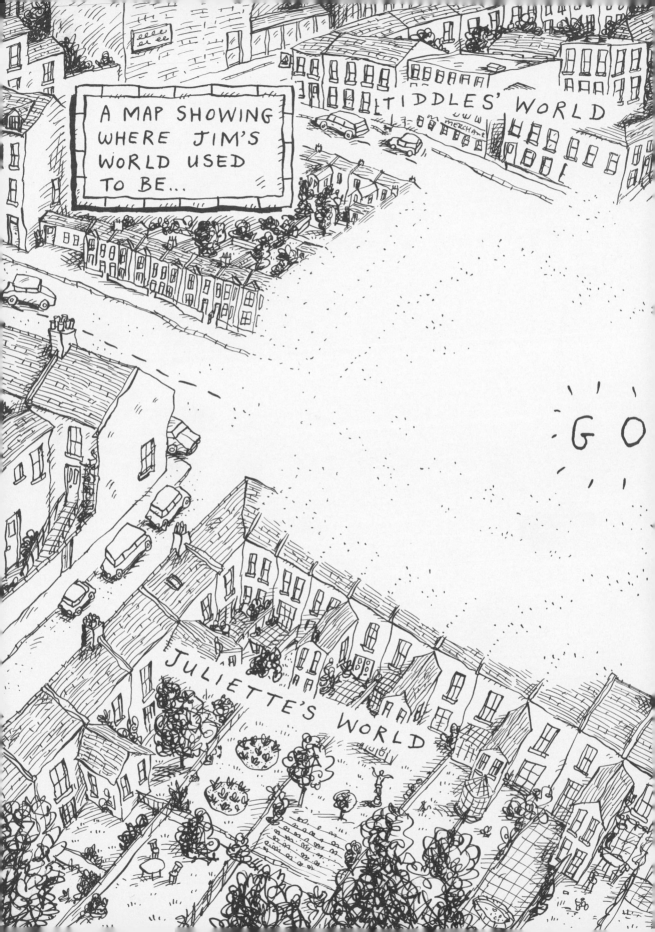